M I N T

MINT

A Book of Recipes

INTRODUCTION BY KATE WHITEMAN

LORENZ BOOKS
NEW YORK • LONDON • SYDNEY • BATH

First published in 1997 by Lorenz Books

© 1997 Anness Publishing Limited

Lorenz Books is an imprint of
Anness Publishing Inc.
27 West 20th Street
New York, NY 10011

ISBN 1 85967 488 7

Publisher Joanna Lorenz
Senior Cookery Editor Linda Fraser
Project Editor Anne Hildyard
Designer Bill Mason
Illustrations Anna Koska

Photographers Karl Adamson, Edward Allwright, James Duncan,
John Freeman, Michelle Garrett and Patrick McLeavey
Recipes Catherine Atkinson, Jacqueline Clark, Joanna Farrow, Christine France,
Shirley Gill, Christine Ingram, Maggie Pannell, Liz Trigg and Steven Wheeler
Food for photography Jacqueline Clark, Joanna Farrow, Katherine Hawins and
Jane Stevenson
Stylists Madeleine Brehaut, Hilary Guy, Blake Minton and Kirsty Rawlings
Jacket photography Janine Hosegood

Printed and bound in China

For all recipes, quantities are given in standard cups and spoons, or, where
appropriate, in imperial measures.

1 3 5 7 9 10 8 6 4 2

Contents

$\mathcal{I}$NTRODUCTION

Intensely fragrant and aromatic, mint is one of the best-known herbs. It takes its name from Minthe, a nymph adored by the Greek god Pluto, and the legend goes that Persephone, Pluto's wife, transformed the nymph into the herb in a fit of jealousy.

Mint has been used throughout the world for centuries, not only in cooking but also as a medicine. It was used for anything, ranging from insomnia to poultices for dog bites and bee stings. Culpeper the herbalist recorded the strange belief that if a wounded man ate mint, he would never recover. In the Middle Ages, mint was valued for its refreshing fragrance and used as a strewing herb in churches, banqueting halls, and bedrooms, and for scenting baths "as a helpe to comfort and strengthen the nerves and sinewes."

A ninth-century monk wrote about the confusing mint varieties: "Mints I grow in abundance and in all its varieties. How many there are, I might as well try to count the sparks from Vulcan's furnace beneath Etna." Today, there are about 25 known species.

Mint is one of the major aromatics in the cuisines of India, Thailand, and the Middle East – just crush a handful of mint and the peppery exotic smell conjures up scenes from an oriental bazaar. The Italians have used mint in their cooking since the days of the Romans, who are thought to have introduced the herb to other parts of Europe.

Mint works best with foods that are already inherently sweet. Roast shoulder of lamb with redcurrant jelly and a vinegary mint sauce is a dish made in heaven. Mint goes well with carrots, parsnips, corn, and peas, and is delicious with sweetly acidic sliced tomatoes dressed with a dribble of olive oil. It will also happily partner fruits – mango, scallion, and mint is a terrific salsa, or try a fruit salad of Charentais melon, grapes, ginger, and mint. Tuck a sprig into a blackberry and apple pie, add it to a quince compote, or even stir it into chocolate mousse to stunning effect.

The recipes in this book draw on a range of cuisines from around the world in which mint has always been a key ingredient. They begin with simple soups and appetizers, including tasty Middle Eastern and Indian dishes. We show how mint can enliven salads and enhance vegetable dishes and then go on to some delicious recipes for fish and seafood. The chapter on meat and poultry includes several inspiring ideas for lamb and mint combinations, as well as others less familiar. We conclude with a mouthwatering selection of minty desserts and irresistible drinks.

Types and Uses of Mint

SPEARMINT *Mentha spicata*
Also known as garden mint or Moroccan mint, this is the most common variety for cooking. The bright green, spear-shaped leaves are deeply veined with toothed edges. They have a strong, clean flavor and are used to season sauces, roast lamb, and other meat dishes and vegetables, especially potatoes and peas.

PEPPERMINT *Mentha piperata*
Peppermint has dark green, sometimes almost purple, intensely aromatic leaves. They produce a pungent oil which is used commercially to flavor confectionery, syrups, toothpaste, liqueurs, and medicines. A steam inhalation of the leaves or their oil will alleviate the symptoms of a head cold or catarrh.

GINGER MINT *Mentha gentilis* "Variegata"
Ginger mint has smooth variegated leaves splashed with yellow. The flavor is mysteriously spicy with a hint of ginger, as the name suggests.

BOWLES' MINT *Mentha rotundifolia*
A variety of applemint, Bowles' mint has apple-scented round, downy leaves with a  beautiful flavor. Less assertive than spearmint or peppermint, it  is delicious in fruit salads and fruit-based drinks.

CATMINT *Nepeta cataria*
A different genus but from the same family as mint, the plant has coarsely toothed, heart-shaped, gray-green leaves with a pungent scent much loved by cats. The leaves can be rubbed onto meat and young shoots can be used sparingly in salads. The leaves are rich in vitamin C and an infusion is said to induce sleep.

DRIED MINT
Being pungent and oily, mint dries more successfully and keeps its flavor longer than more delicate herbs. Dried mint can be used in cooking and to make teas. Store it in an airtight dark glass jar away from heat.

MINT JELLY
Mint jelly is good with all kinds of hot or cold meats and poultry, particularly roast lamb.

MINT SAUCE
The acidity of the vinegar in this traditional English sauce cuts the sweetness of lamb.

Dried mint

Mint sauce

Mint jelly

Catmint

Ginger mint

Peppermint

Spearmint

Bowles' mint

$\mathscr{B}$ASIC $\mathscr{T}$ECHNIQUES

USING MINT

• *Buying:* Choose healthy-looking sprigs with a good fragrance. Avoid wilted specimens with dried ends, brown leaves, or where the leaves drop when shaken.

• *Picking:* Harvest fresh mint just before flowering when the flavor is at its peak. The best time to pick is in the morning after the dew has evaporated. Avoid washing the leaves unless absolutely necessary.

• *Storing:* Wrap in damp kitchen paper and store in a plastic bag in the salad drawer of the refrigerator. Put large bunches in a pitcher of water and loosely cover with a plastic bag. Keep out of direct sunlight.

• *Freezing:* Frozen mint is too limp to be used as a garnish but it can be added to soups, sauces, and herb butters. Rinse and thoroughly dry the sprigs and pack them flat in small plastic boxes. Snip or grate as required from the frozen clump. Alternatively, chop finely and freeze in ice cube trays.

• *Garnishing:* Sprinkle fresh mint over salads, soups, and vegetables at the last minute for maximum flavor.

• *Growing:* Mint always gets out of control if left to its own devices. Even if you hard prune or pull it up, mint always comes back. To prevent rampant root growth, imprison your mint in an old earthenware sink, or a pail embedded in the soil.

MINT SAUCE

Strip a good-size handful of fresh mint leaves from the stems and chop the leaves very finely.

Pound the chopped leaves with 1–2 tsp superfine sugar.

Stir in 2 tbsp boiling water. Add 2 tbsp vinegar and leave to stand for about 30 minutes.

COOK'S TIPS

• *Mint tea:* Put a handful of fresh mint leaves in a teapot or heatproof pitcher. Pour over 2½ cups boiling water, cover, and leave for 5 minutes, then strain into cups. Sweeten with either clear honey or sugar if liked.

• *Mint butter:* Cream ½ cup sweet butter with 2 tbsp chopped mint, 1 tbsp lemon juice, and salt and pepper.

• *Candied mint leaves:* Choose perfect leaves that are completely dry. Lightly whisk egg white until it is just sloppy. With a fine paintbrush, coat the leaves evenly with a thin layer of egg white. Dust lightly with superfine sugar. Place on a wire rack to dry.

• *Mint liqueur:* Shake together 1oz chopped mint leaves and 1 bottle brandy. Seal and store in the dark for a week, shaking daily. Strain, add 2 cups superfine sugar, 1 tbsp glycerin, and a little green food coloring. Bottle and seal.

PUY LENTIL, MINT AND LEMON SALAD   Serves 4

Rinse 8oz lentils and put in a saucepan with about 2½ cups water. Bring to a boil and simmer briskly for 15 minutes until just tender and still holding their shape. Drain and tip into a serving bowl. While the lentils are still warm, stir in 1 crushed garlic clove, the juice of 1–1½ lemons, ½ tsp cumin seeds, 4 tbsp olive oil, 3–4 tbsp chopped fresh mint, salt, and freshly ground black pepper and mix gently until thoroughly combined. Garnish with lemon wedges and a few sprigs of fresh mint and serve the salad warm.

Soups and Appetizers

Versatile and refreshing, fresh mint makes an aromatic addition to all types of first courses. It can bring the simplest soup to life and is particularly good in Middle Eastern dishes.

MINTED MELON AND GRAPEFRUIT

Melon is always a popular appetizer. Here the delicate flavor is complemented by the refreshing taste of citrus fruit and mint with a deliciously piquant sweet-and-sour dressing.

Serves 4

*1 small cantaloupe melon, weighing
   about 2¼lb*

2 pink grapefruits

1 yellow grapefruit

1 tsp Dijon mustard

1 tsp raspberry or sherry vinegar

1 tsp honey

1 tbsp chopped fresh mint

sprigs of fresh mint, to garnish

COOK'S TIP

*If you do not have a melon
baller, cut the melon flesh from
the rind, and then dice into
neat cubes with a knife.*

Halve the melon and remove the seeds with a teaspoon. With a melon baller, carefully scoop the flesh into balls.

With a sharp knife, peel the grapefruits and remove all the white pith. Segment the flesh by cutting between the membranes, holding the fruit over a small bowl to catch any juices.

Whisk the mustard, vinegar, honey, chopped mint, and grapefruit juices together in a mixing bowl. Add the melon balls, together with the grapefruit, and mix well. Chill for 30 minutes.

Ladle into four dishes and serve garnished with a sprig of fresh mint.

SHRIMP WITH FRESH MINT VINAIGRETTE

Mint and lemon balm make a subtle combination to create a perfect balance with the exotic, tropical flavor of mango in this deceptively simple appetizer.

Serves 4

1 large mango
8oz extra-large cooked shrimp, peeled and deveined
16 cherry tomatoes, halved
sprigs of fresh mint, to garnish

For the dressing

1 tbsp white wine vinegar
½ tsp clear honey
1 tbsp mango or apricot chutney
1 tbsp chopped fresh mint
1 tbsp chopped fresh lemon balm
3 tbsp olive oil
salt and ground black pepper

COOK'S TIP

If you use frozen shrimp, thaw them in a strainer and drain on paper towels before use or the water will dilute the salad dressing and spoil the flavor.

Using a sharp knife, peel, pit, and dice the mango carefully. Mix with the shrimp and cherry tomatoes in a bowl. Toss lightly to mix, then cover, and chill.

Make the salad dressing by mixing the vinegar, clear honey, mango or apricot chutney, and fresh herbs in a bowl. Gradually whisk in the oil, then add salt and pepper to taste.

Spoon the shrimp mixture into the dressing and toss lightly, then divide among serving dishes. Garnish with the fresh mint sprigs and serve.

MINTED YOGURT AND CUCUMBER SOUP

Mint brings an extra lift to this creamy Middle Eastern-style cold soup – perfect for a summer lunch.

Serves 4

1 large cucumber, peeled

1¼ cups light cream

⅔ cup natural yogurt

2 garlic cloves, crushed

2 tbsp white wine vinegar

1 tbsp chopped fresh mint

salt and ground black pepper

sprigs of fresh mint, to garnish

Grate the cucumber coarsely. Place in a bowl with the cream, yogurt, garlic, vinegar, and mint. Stir well and season to taste.

Chill for at least 2 hours. Just before serving, stir the soup again. Pour into individual bowls and garnish with mint sprigs.

LAMB TIKKA IN MINT MARINADE

Creamy yogurt and nuts go wonderfully with the spices and mint in these little Indian meatballs.

Makes about 20
1lb lamb fillet
2 scallions, chopped

For the marinade
1½ cups natural yogurt
1 tbsp ground almonds, cashews, or
*   peanuts*
1 tbsp vegetable oil
2–3 garlic cloves, finely chopped
juice of 1 lemon
1 tsp garam masala or
*   curry powder*
½ tsp ground cardamom
¼ tsp cayenne pepper
1–2 tbsp chopped fresh mint

Prepare the marinade by mixing all the ingredients together in a medium-size bowl. In a separate small bowl, reserve about ½ cup of the mixture to use as a dipping sauce.

Cut the lamb into small pieces and put in the bowl of a food processor with the scallions. Process, using the pulse action, until the meat is finely chopped. Add 2–3 tbsp of the marinade and process again.

Test to see if the mixture holds together by pinching a little between your fingertips. Add a little more marinade if necessary, but do not make the mixture too wet and soft.

With moistened palms, form the meat mixture into slightly oval-shaped balls about 1½in long and arrange in a shallow dish. Spoon over the remaining marinade and chill the meatballs in the refrigerator for 8–10 hours or overnight.

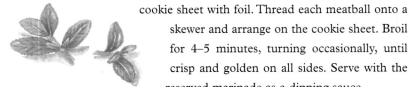

When you are ready to cook, preheat the broiler and line a cookie sheet with foil. Thread each meatball onto a skewer and arrange on the cookie sheet. Broil for 4–5 minutes, turning occasionally, until crisp and golden on all sides. Serve with the reserved marinade as a dipping sauce.

Salads and Vegetable Dishes

Brighten the flavor of salads with fresh mint
instead of basil or parsley. Used in generous
amounts, mint gives an exotic touch and fresh
taste to grain-based salads and also
lightens the texture.

FATTOUSH

This simple and colorful peasant salad, in which mint blends with a mixture of other fresh herbs, is a popular dish throughout Syria and the Lebanon.

Serves 4

1 yellow or red bell pepper

1 large cucumber

4–5 tomatoes

1 bunch scallions

2 tbsp finely chopped fresh mint

2 tbsp finely chopped fresh parsley

2 tbsp finely chopped fresh cilantro

2 garlic cloves, crushed

5 tbsp olive oil

juice of 2 lemons

salt and ground black pepper

2 pitta breads, to serve

S lice the bell pepper, discarding the seeds and core, then roughly chop the cucumber and tomatoes. Place them in a large salad bowl.

Trim and slice the scallions. Add to the cucumber, tomatoes, and pepper with the finely chopped mint, parsley, and cilantro.

To make the dressing, blend the garlic with the olive oil and lemon juice in a pitcher, then season to taste with salt and black pepper. Pour the dressing over the salad and toss lightly to mix.

Toast the pitta breads in a toaster or under a hot broiler until crisp and serve them alongside the salad.

COOK'S TIP

Traditionally, the pitta bread is toasted until crisp, crushed in the hand, and then sprinkled over the salad before serving.

COOL MINT RAITA

This refreshing minty dish is the ideal antidote to any spicy food, especially fiery Indian curries.

Serves 4

7 large fresh mint sprigs

1 small onion

$\frac{1}{2}$ cucumber

$1\frac{1}{4}$ cups natural yogurt

$\frac{1}{2}$ tsp salt

$\frac{1}{2}$ tsp sugar

pinch of chili powder

COOK'S TIP

This also makes a deliciously fresh dip for crudités. Use Greek-style yogurt for a creamier texture and add some crushed garlic for extra flavor. Serve with raw fresh vegetables cut into matchstick strips or tortilla chips.

Tear the leaves from the stalks of 6 of the mint sprigs and chop finely. Peel and very thinly slice the onion, separating it into rings. Cut the cucumber into $\frac{1}{4}$in dice.

Mix together the chopped mint, onion, cucumber, yogurt, salt, and sugar. Spoon into a serving bowl and chill.

Just before serving sprinkle with chili powder and garnish with the remaining mint sprig.

TZATZIKI

Tzatziki is a Greek cucumber salad dressed with yogurt, mint, and garlic. It is typically served with broiled lamb and chicken, but is also good with salmon and trout.

Serves 4

1 cucumber

1 tsp salt

3 tbsp finely chopped fresh mint, plus a few sprigs to garnish

1 garlic clove, crushed

1 tsp superfine sugar

1 cup strained Greek-style yogurt

paprika, to garnish (optional)

Peel the cucumber. Reserve a little to use as a garnish if you wish and cut the rest in half lengthwise. Remove the seeds with a teaspoon and discard. Slice the cucumber thinly and combine with the salt. Leave for approximately 15–20 minutes. Salt will soften the cucumber and draw out any bitter juices.

Combine the chopped mint, garlic, sugar, and yogurt in a bowl.

Thoroughly rinse the cucumber in a strainer under plenty of cold running water to flush away the salt. Drain well and combine with the yogurt. Garnish with the reserved cucumber, if using, and the mint sprigs and sprinkle with paprika if you wish.

COOK'S TIP

If you are preparing tzatziki in a hurry, do not stop to dégorge the cucumber (that is the salting process). The cucumber will have a somewhat crunchier texture and will also be slightly less sweet.

ZUCCHINI MINT PUFFS WITH SALAD

These unusual light puffs, made of grated zucchini flavored with mint, are served warm on a bed of mixed salad greens with a balsamic dressing.

Serves 2

1lb zucchini

1½ cups fresh white breadcrumbs

1 egg

pinch of cayenne pepper

1 tbsp chopped fresh mint

oil, for deep-frying

1 tbsp balsamic vinegar

3 tbsp extra virgin olive oil

7oz mixed salad greens

salt and ground black pepper

Top and tail the zucchini. Coarsely grate them and put into a colander. Squeeze out the excess water, then put the zucchini into a bowl. Add the breadcrumbs, egg, cayenne, mint, and seasoning. Mix well. Shape the zucchini mixture into balls about the size of walnuts.

Heat the oil for deep-frying to 350°F or until a cube of bread, when added to the oil, browns in 30–40 seconds. Deep-fry the zucchini balls in batches for 2–3 minutes. Drain on paper towels.

Whisk the vinegar and olive oil together and season well. Put the salad greens in a bowl and pour over the dressing. Add the zucchini puffs and toss lightly together. Serve at once, while the zucchini puffs are still crisp.

COOK'S TIP

Choose a colorful and decorative mixture of salad greens to accompany this attractive vegetable dish.

MINTED EGG AND FENNEL TABBOULEH

Tabbouleh, a Middle Eastern dish of steamed cracked wheat, is ideal for warm-weather picnics.

Serves 4

1½ cups cracked wheat

2 eggs

1 fennel bulb

1 bunch scallions, chopped

1oz sun-dried tomatoes, sliced

2 tbsp chopped fresh mint

3 tbsp chopped fresh parsley

3oz black olives

6 tbsp olive oil, preferably Greek or
*   Spanish*

2 tbsp lemon juice

1 Romaine lettuce

50g/2oz chopped hazelnuts, toasted

salt and ground black pepper

1 medium open-textured loaf or 4
*   pitta breads, warmed, to serve*

Put the cracked wheat in a large bowl and cover with boiling water. Set aside to soak for 15 minutes. Transfer to a metal strainer, position over a saucepan of boiling water, cover, and steam for 10 minutes. Spread out on a metal tray and leave to cool.

Hard-cook the eggs for 12 minutes. Cool under running water, shell, and quarter. Halve and finely slice the fennel. Boil in salted water for 6 minutes, drain, and cool under running water. Combine the eggs, fennel, scallions, sun-dried tomatoes, mint, parsley, and olives with the cracked wheat. Dress with the olive oil and lemon juice. Season well.

Wash the lettuce leaves and spin dry. Line an attractive salad bowl or plate with the leaves, pile in the tabbouleh, and scatter with toasted hazelnuts. Serve with a basket of warm bread.

CRACKED WHEAT SALAD WITH MINT

Rich in protein, cracked wheat makes an excellent alternative to rice or pasta.

Serves 4

¾ cup cracked wheat

2½ cups water

1 small green bell pepper

¼ cucumber, diced

½ cup chopped fresh mint

⅓ cup flaked almonds, toasted

grated rind and juice of 1 lemon

2 seedless oranges

salt and ground black pepper

sprigs of fresh mint, to garnish

Place the cracked wheat in a saucepan and add the water. Bring to a boil, lower the heat, cover, and simmer for 10–15 minutes until tender. Alternatively, place the cracked wheat in a heatproof bowl, pour over boiling water, and leave to soak for 30 minutes. Most, if not all, of the water should be absorbed; drain off any excess, and allow to cool.

Using a vegetable knife, halve, core, and seed the green bell pepper and cut it into small cubes.

Toss the cracked wheat with the cucumber, green bell pepper, mint, and toasted almonds in a serving bowl. Add the grated lemon rind and juice.

Cut the rind from the oranges, then, working over the bowl to catch the juice, cut the oranges into neat segments. Add to the cracked wheat mixture, then season, and toss lightly. Garnish with the mint sprigs.

SMOKED TROUT WITH MINT MAYONNAISE

Trout and grapefruit make a magical combination – especially with an added hint of mint.

Serves 4

1 lollo rosso lettuce

1 tbsp lemon juice

2 tbsp chopped fresh mint, plus a few whole leaves to garnish

1lb smoked trout, skinned, boned, and sliced

2 grapefruits, peeled and segmented

½ cup good-quality mayonnaise

Toss the lettuce with the lemon juice and half the chopped mint. Arrange on a plate and place the smoked trout among the leaves. Arrange the grapefruit segments decoratively on the salad.

Mix the remaining chopped mint with the mayonnaise and serve separately in a small bowl, garnished with a mint leaf or two.

SPICED EGGPLANT WITH MINT YOGURT

A minty yogurt sauce is the perfect complement to eggplants cooked with mixed spices.

Serves 4

2–3 eggplants

2–3 tbsp olive oil

1 tsp ground cumin

1 tsp ground coriander

¼ tsp chili powder

⅔ cup Greek-style yogurt

1 garlic clove, crushed

2 tbsp chopped fresh mint, plus extra
   to garnish

salt and ground black pepper

COOK'S TIP

*Dégorging or salting the
eggplant slices helps to extract
the bitter juices.*

Slice the eggplants thickly and place in a shallow dish. Sprinkle with salt and leave to drain for 30 minutes. Rinse the eggplant slices and pat dry thoroughly with kitchen paper.

Arrange the eggplants on a cookie sheet and brush with oil. Sprinkle over half of each spice. Cook under a hot broiler until soft and browned.

Turn over the eggplant slices, brush again with oil, and sprinkle with the remaining spices. Broil for a further 4–5 minutes, until the second sides are browned.

Meanwhile, make the mint yogurt. Mix together the yogurt, crushed garlic, and mint and season to taste with plenty of freshly ground black pepper. Spoon into a small serving bowl.

Arrange the broiled eggplants on a serving plate, sprinkle with chopped mint, and serve with the mint yogurt.

VEGETABLE FRITTERS WITH MINT SALSA

The Thai-style mint salsa goes just as well with plain stir-fried salmon strips or stir-fried beef as it does with these melt-in-the-mouth zucchini fritters.

Serves 2–3

2 tsp cumin seeds

2 tsp coriander seeds

1 cup garbanzo-bean flour

½ cup peanut oil

1lb zucchini

salt and ground black pepper

sprigs of fresh mint, to garnish

For the mint salsa

½ cucumber, diced

3 scallions, chopped

6 radishes, cubed

2 tbsp chopped fresh mint

*1in fresh ginger root, peeled
    and grated*

3 tbsp lime juice

2 tbsp superfine sugar

3 garlic cloves, crushed

Heat a wok or heavy-based skillet, then toast the cumin and coriander seeds. Cool them, then grind well, using a pestle and mortar.

Blend the garbanzo-bean flour, spices, and salt and pepper in a food processor. Add ½ cup warm water with 1 tbsp peanut oil, and blend again.

Cut the zucchini into 3in sticks. Place in a bowl. Coat the zucchini in the batter, then leave to stand for 10 minutes.

To make the mint salsa, mix all the ingredients together in a bowl until thoroughly combined and set aside.

Heat the wok or skillet, then add the remaining oil. When the oil is hot, stir-fry the zucchini in batches. Drain well on paper towels, then serve hot with the salsa, garnished with fresh mint sprigs.

BAKED ZUCCHINI WITH MINT

Creamy yet tangy goat's cheese combines with fresh mint to make simple baked zucchini into a special dish.

Serves 4

*8 small zucchini, weighing about 1lb
in total*

*1 tbsp olive oil, plus extra
for greasing*

*3–4oz goat's cheese, cut into thin
strips*

*1 small bunch fresh mint,
finely chopped*

ground black pepper

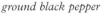

COOK'S TIP

*The many different types of
goat's cheese vary from smooth
and fresh-tasting to very strong
and tangy, but if you don't like
the flavor, you could substitute
a milder cheese, such as
mozzarella, Pecorino or mild
Cheddar.*

Preheat the oven to 350°F. Cut out eight rectangles of foil large enough to encase each zucchini and brush each with a little oil.

Trim the zucchini and cut a thin slit along the length of each. Insert pieces of goat's cheese in the slits. Add a little mint and sprinkle with the olive oil and black pepper.

Wrap each zucchini in a foil rectangle, place on a cookie sheet, and bake for about 25 minutes until tender.

MINTED COUSCOUS CASTLES

Couscous, a fine semolina made from wheat grain, is usually steamed and served plain with a rich meat or vegetable stew. Here it is flavored with mint and molded to make an unusual accompaniment to serve with any meat-based or vegetarian savory dish.

Serves 6

1⅓ *cups couscous*

2 *cups boiling stock*

1 *tbsp lemon juice*

2 *tomatoes, diced*

2 *tbsp chopped fresh mint*

oil, for brushing

salt and ground black pepper

sprigs of fresh mint, to garnish

COOK'S TIP

Most commercially produced couscous is now the ready-cooked variety, which can be cooked as described here, but some types need steaming first, so you should always check the pack instructions.

Place the couscous in a bowl and pour over the boiling stock. Cover the bowl and leave to stand for 30 minutes, until all the stock is absorbed and the grains are tender.

Stir in the lemon juice with the tomatoes and chopped mint. Season to taste with salt and pepper.

Brush the sides of your cups or individual molds with oil. Spoon in the couscous mixture and pack down firmly. Chill for several hours.

Turn out and serve cold. Alternatively, cover and heat gently in a low oven or microwave, then turn out, and serve hot. Either way, garnish with mint.

FRESH MINTED VEGETABLE STEW

A spiced dish of mixed vegetables, with the addition of fresh mint, this aromatic stew can be served as a side dish or as a vegetarian main course.

Serves 4–6

3 tbsp vegetable stock

1 green bell pepper, seeded and sliced

2 medium zucchini, sliced

2 medium carrots, sliced

2 celery stalks, sliced

2 medium potatoes, diced

14oz can chopped tomatoes

1 tsp chili powder

2 tbsp chopped fresh mint

1 tbsp ground cumin

14oz can garbanzo beans, drained

salt and ground black pepper

fresh mint leaves, to garnish

COOK'S TIP

Garbanzo beans are traditional in this type of Middle Eastern dish, but if you prefer, kidney beans or navy beans can be used instead.

Heat the vegetable stock in a large flameproof casserole until boiling, then add the sliced bell pepper, zucchini, carrots, and celery. Stir over a high heat for 2–3 minutes, until the vegetables are beginning to soften.

Add the potatoes, tomatoes, chili powder, mint, and cumin. Add the garbanzo beans and bring to a boil.

Reduce the heat, cover the casserole, and simmer for 30 minutes, or until all the vegetables are tender. Season to taste with salt and pepper and serve hot, garnished with mint leaves.

Vegetables with Cider and Mint

The cider sauce is also ideal for other vegetables, such as celery or beans. It is flavored with tamari, a Japanese soy sauce, and applemint.

Serves 4

1 large onion, chopped

2 large carrots, chopped

1 large garlic clove

1 tbsp dill seeds

4 large applemint sprigs

2 tbsp olive oil

2 tbsp all-purpose flour

1¼ cups hard cider

1lb broccoli flowerets

1lb cauliflower flowerets

2 tbsp tamari

2 tsp mint jelly

Sauté the onion, carrots, garlic, dill seeds, and applemint in the olive oil until the vegetables are nearly cooked. Stir in the flour and cook for about 30 seconds. Pour in the cider and simmer until the sauce looks glossy.

Boil the broccoli and cauliflower in separate pans until tender.

Pour the sauce into a food processor and add the tamari and the mint jelly. Blend until finely puréed. Drain the broccoli and cauliflower and transfer to a serving dish. Pour over the sauce and serve.

Fish and Seafood

Combined with other ingredients, such as spices and zesty citrus fruits, mint gets the taste buds tingling and adds a refreshing clean flavor to marinades and sauces for fish and shellfish.

MINTY COD PLAKI

A wonderful Greek recipe in which cod is cooked gently in olive oil with onions and tomatoes flavored with mint and other fresh aromatic herbs.

Serves 6

1¼ cups olive oil

2 onions, thinly sliced

2 large well-flavored tomatoes,
    roughly chopped

3 garlic cloves, thinly sliced

1 tsp sugar

1 tsp chopped fresh mint

1 tsp chopped fresh dill

1 tsp chopped fresh celery leaves

1 tbsp chopped fresh parsley

1¼ cups water

6 cod steaks

juice of 1 lemon

salt and ground black pepper

sprigs of fresh mint, to garnish

Heat the oil in a large skillet or flameproof dish. Add the onions and cook until pale golden and softened. Add the tomatoes, garlic, sugar, mint, dill, celery leaves, and parsley with the water. Season with salt and pepper, then simmer, uncovered, for 25 minutes, until the liquid has reduced by about one-third.

Add the fish steaks and cook gently for 10–12 minutes, until the fish is just cooked. Remove from the heat and add the lemon juice. Cover and leave to stand for about 20 minutes before serving. Arrange the cod in a dish and spoon the sauce over. Garnish with mint and serve warm or cold.

MINTED PORGY

Pine kernels, raisins, and cinnamon mingle with mint in this Middle Eastern dish.

Serves 4

4lb whole porgy or 2 smaller porgy

2 tbsp olive oil

¾ cup pine kernels

1 large onion, finely chopped

1lb ripe tomatoes, roughly chopped

½ cup raisins

¼ tsp ground cinnamon

¼ tsp ground apple pie spice

3 tbsp chopped fresh mint

1 cup long-grain rice

3 lemon slices

1¼ cups fish stock

salt

Trim, gut, and scale the fish or ask your fish store to do this for you. Preheat the oven to 350°F.

Heat the oil in a large, heavy-based saucepan and stir-fry the pine kernels for 1 minute. Add the onion and continue to stir-fry until it is soft but not colored. Add the tomatoes and simmer for 10 minutes.

Stir in the raisins, most of the cinnamon and apple pie spice, the mint, rice, and lemon slices. Transfer the mixture to a large roasting pan and pour over the stock. Arrange the fish on top and cut several diagonal slashes in the skin with a sharp knife. Sprinkle over a little salt, the remaining cinnamon and apple pie spice, and bake in the oven for 30–35 minutes for the large fish or 20–25 minutes for the smaller fish.

COOK'S TIP

Porgy is a large family of fish and all varieties are equally delicious. Black and red porgy and daurade are the most readily available.

SPICED MINT RAINBOW TROUT

Rainbow trout fillets coated in a minty marinade make a tasty, quick meal when broiled or barbecued.

Serves 4

*4 large rainbow trout fillets, about
  5oz each*

1 tbsp ground coriander

1 garlic clove, crushed

2 tbsp finely chopped fresh mint

1 tsp paprika

¾ cup natural yogurt

salad and pitta bread, to serve

With a sharp knife, slash the flesh of the fish fillets through the skin fairly deeply at intervals.

Mix together the coriander, garlic, mint, paprika, and yogurt. Spread this mixture evenly over the fish and leave to marinate for about an hour.

Cook the fish under a preheated moderately hot broiler or on a barbecue, turning occasionally, until crisp and golden. Serve hot with a crisp salad and some warmed pitta bread.

Nowadays, rainbow trout are mainly farmed fish and extra flavoring is usually essential to bring out the best in them. However, the delicious combination of coriander, mint, and yogurt would also suit the more delicate flavor of brown trout, if you are lucky enough to find them. In this case, garlic may be too robust and is probably better omitted.

COOK'S TIP

If you are using the broiler rather than the barbecue, it is best to line the broiler pan with foil before cooking the trout.

SHRIMP AND MINT SALAD

Serving the shrimp warm enhances the minty flavor and appetizing aroma of their sauce.

Serves 4

12 large raw shrimp

1 tbsp sweet butter

1 tbsp fish sauce

juice of 1 lime

3 tbsp thin coconut milk

1 tsp superfine sugar

1 garlic clove, crushed

1in fresh ginger root, peeled
    and grated

2 red chilies, seeded and
    finely chopped

2 tbsp fresh mint leaves

8oz light green lettuce leaves

ground black pepper

fresh coconut shavings, to
    garnish (optional)

Peel the shrimp and remove the heads, leaving the tails intact. Remove the dark vein running down the back of each shrimp. If you are using frozen raw shrimp, allow them to thaw completely first. (If you are using crayfish, remove the heads and hard shells with a knife. Lobster tails will require no extra preparation.)

Melt the butter in a large, heavy-based skillet and toss the shrimp in it until they have all turned pink. Make sure that they are all thoroughly cooked, as eating undercooked shrimp can be dangerous.

Mix the fish sauce, lime juice, coconut milk, sugar, garlic, ginger, chilies, and pepper together.

Toss the warm shrimp in the sauce with the mint leaves. Arrange a bed of lettuce leaves on a serving platter and top with the warm shrimp and sauce. Garnish, if you wish, with fresh coconut shavings and serve.

COOK'S TIP

Lobster tails or crayfish make elegant substitutes for the shrimp if you are feeling extravagant.

Meat and Poultry

Meat and mint are perfect partners. The classic combination of lamb and mint is particularly delicious. Mint is good with poultry too; try using some of the more unusual varieties, such as applemint and ginger mint.

LAMB AND MINT KHORESH

Mint brings a lovely fresh taste and delicious fragrance to this unusual stew.

Serves 4

1 large onion, chopped

3 tbsp butter

1lb lean lamb, cubed

1 tsp ground turmeric

½ tsp ground cinnamon

2½ cups water

1 head celery, chopped

1 small bunch fresh mint, chopped

1oz fresh parsley, chopped

juice of 1 lemon

salt and ground black pepper

mint leaves, to garnish

cooked rice, and cucumber and
    tomato salad, to serve

COOK'S TIP

*If you prefer, this dish can be
made with canned or chopped
fresh plum tomatoes in place of
some of the herbs. Add the
tomatoes at the same time as
the celery.*

Fry the onion in 2 tbsp of the butter in a large saucepan or flameproof casserole for 3–4 minutes. Add the meat and cook for 2–3 minutes until browned, stirring frequently, then stir in the turmeric, cinnamon, and salt and pepper.

Add the water and bring to a boil, then reduce the heat, cover, and simmer for about 30 minutes until the meat is half-cooked.

Melt the remaining butter in a skillet and fry the celery for 8–10 minutes, until tender, stirring frequently. Add the mint and parsley and fry for a further 3–4 minutes.

Stir the celery and herbs, together with the lemon juice, into the meat and simmer, covered, for a further 25–30 minutes until the meat is completely tender. Serve garnished with mint leaves and accompanied by cooked rice and a cucumber and tomato salad.

LEBANESE KIBBEH WITH MINTED DIP

Kibbeh is a kind of Middle Eastern meatloaf made from ground lamb and cracked wheat, here served with a creamy minted yogurt dip.

Serves 6

⅔ cup cracked wheat
1lb finely ground lean lamb
1 large onion, grated
1 tbsp melted butter
salt and ground black pepper
sprigs of fresh mint, to garnish
cooked rice, to serve

For the filling

2 tbsp oil
1 onion, finely chopped
8oz ground lamb or veal
½ cup pine kernels
½ tsp ground allspice

For the yogurt dip

2½ cups Greek-style yogurt
2–3 garlic cloves, crushed
1–2 tbsp chopped fresh mint

Preheat the oven to 375°F. Rinse the cracked wheat in a strainer and squeeze out the excess moisture.

Mix the lamb, onion, and seasoning, kneading the mixture to make a thick paste. Add the cracked wheat and blend together.

To make the filling, heat the oil in a skillet and fry the onion until golden. Add the lamb or veal and cook, stirring, until evenly browned. Add the pine kernels, allspice, and salt and pepper.

Oil a large baking dish and spread half of the meat and cracked wheat mixture over the bottom. Spoon over the filling and top with a second layer of meat and cracked wheat, pressing down firmly with the back of a spoon. Pour the melted butter over the top and bake in the oven for 40–45 minutes until browned on top.

Meanwhile make the yogurt dip: blend together the yogurt and garlic, spoon into a serving bowl, and sprinkle with the chopped mint.

Cut the cooked kibbeh into squares or rectangles and serve garnished with mint sprigs and accompanied by cooked rice and the yogurt dip.

MINTY LAMB BURGERS

These rather special burgers, flavored with mint and stuffed with melting mozzarella cheese, take a little extra time to prepare, but are well worth it. Redcurrant chutney makes an unusual accompaniment.

Serves 4

1¼lb lean ground lamb

1 small onion, finely chopped

2 tbsp finely chopped fresh mint

2 tbsp finely chopped fresh parsley

4oz mozzarella cheese

salt and ground black pepper

oil, for brushing

For the chutney

1½ cups fresh or frozen redcurrants

2 tsp clear honey

1 tsp balsamic vinegar

2 tbsp finely chopped fresh mint

Mix together the lamb, onion, mint, and parsley until evenly combined; season well with salt and pepper. Divide the mixture into eight equal pieces and use your hands to press them into flat rounds.

Cut the mozzarella into 4 slices or cubes. Place them on 4 of the lamb rounds. Top each with another round of meat mixture. Press together firmly, making 4 flattish burger shapes and sealing in the cheese completely.

Place all the ingredients for the chutney in a bowl and mash them together with a fork. Season well with salt and pepper.

Brush the lamb patties with oil and cook them over a moderately hot barbecue for about 15 minutes, turning once, until golden brown. Serve with the redcurrant chutney.

LAMB AND LEEKS WITH MINT

Mint adds an extra dimension to this lamb and leek casserole nestling beneath a potato topping.

Serves 6

2 tbsp sunflower oil

4lb lamb (fillet or boned leg), cubed

10 scallions, thickly sliced

3 leeks, thickly sliced

1 tbsp flour

⅔ cup white wine

1¼ cups chicken stock

1 tbsp tomato paste

1 tbsp sugar

2 tbsp finely chopped fresh mint

1 cup dried pears, chopped

2lb potatoes, sliced

2 tbsp melted butter

salt and ground black pepper

fresh mint leaves, to garnish

Preheat the oven to 350°F.

Heat the oil and fry the lamb to seal it. Transfer to a casserole.

Fry the scallions and leeks for 1 minute, stir in the flour, and cook for another minute. Add the wine and stock and bring to a boil. Add the tomato paste, sugar, salt, and pepper with the mint and pears and pour into the casserole. Stir the mixture. Arrange the sliced potatoes on top and brush with the melted butter.

Cover the casserole and bake in the oven for 1½ hours. Then increase the temperature to 400°F and cook for a further 30 minutes, uncovered, to brown the potatoes. Garnish with mint leaves before serving.

MINTED KOFTAS IN TOMATO SAUCE

There are many varieties of koftas – Middle Eastern meatballs – and this popular version uses mint.

Serves 4

12oz ground lamb or beef

½ cup fresh breadcrumbs

1 onion, grated

3 tbsp chopped fresh parsley

1 tbsp chopped fresh mint

1 tsp ground cumin

1 tsp ground turmeric

3 tbsp oil

salt and ground black pepper

fresh mint leaves, to garnish

egg noodles, to serve

For the tomato sauce

1 tbsp oil

1 onion, chopped

14oz can plum tomatoes

1 tsp tomato paste

juice of ½ lemon

First make the tomato sauce. Heat the oil in a large saucepan or flameproof casserole and fry the onion until golden. Stir in the canned tomatoes, tomato paste, lemon juice, and seasoning. Bring to a boil, reduce the heat, and simmer for about 10 minutes.

Meanwhile, place the ground lamb or beef in a large bowl and mix in the breadcrumbs, grated onion, herbs and spices, and a little salt and pepper. Knead the mixture by hand until thoroughly blended and then shape into walnut-size balls.

Heat the oil in a skillet and fry the meatballs, in batches if necessary, until browned. Transfer them to the tomato sauce, cover, and simmer for about 30 minutes. Garnish with mint leaves and serve with noodles.

MINTED LAMB SKEWERS

The perfect partnership of lamb and mint triumphs again in this recipe.

Serves 4

1¼ cups Greek-style yogurt

½ garlic clove, crushed

good pinch of saffron powder

2 tbsp chopped fresh mint

2 tbsp clear honey

3 tbsp olive oil

3 lamb neck fillets, about 1½lb

1 medium eggplant

2 small red onions, quartered

salt and ground black pepper

sprigs of fresh mint, to garnish

mixed salad and hot pitta bread,
    to serve

In a shallow dish, mix together the yogurt, garlic, saffron, mint, honey, oil, and black pepper. Trim the lamb and cut into 1in cubes. Add to the marinade and stir until well coated. Cover and leave to marinate for at least 4 hours, or preferably overnight.

Cut the eggplant into 1in cubes and blanch in boiling salted water for 1–2 minutes. Drain well and pat dry on paper towels.

Remove the lamb cubes from the marinade. Thread the lamb, eggplant, and onion pieces alternately onto skewers. Broil for 10–12 minutes under a preheated broiler, turning and basting occasionally with the marinade, until the lamb is tender.

Serve the skewers garnished with mint sprigs, and accompanied by a mixed salad and hot pitta bread.

COOK'S TIP

If you are using bamboo skewers, soak them in cold water before use to prevent them burning.

MINTY YOGURT CHICKEN

The subtle spicy flavor of ginger mint adds a hint of the Orient to this succulent marinated chicken.

Serves 4

8 chicken thigh portions, skinned

1 tbsp clear honey

2 tbsp lime or lemon juice

2 tbsp natural yogurt

4 tbsp chopped fresh mint, preferably ginger mint

salt and ground black pepper

boiled potatoes and tomato salad, to serve

Slash the chicken flesh at intervals with a sharp knife. Place in a bowl. In another bowl mix together the honey, lime or lemon juice, yogurt, seasoning, and half the mint.

Spoon the marinade over the chicken and leave to marinate for 30 minutes. Line the broiler pan with foil and cook the chicken under a preheated moderately hot broiler until thoroughly cooked and golden brown, turning occasionally.

Sprinkle the chicken with the remaining mint to garnish and serve with boiled potatoes and tomato salad.

TURKEY WITH FIGS AND MINT

This unusual fruit and mint sauce gives a tremendous lift to the rather bland flavor of turkey.

Serves 4

1lb dried figs

½ bottle sweet, fruity white wine

1 tbsp butter

4 turkey fillets, 6–8oz each

2 tbsp dark orange marmalade

*10 fresh mint leaves, preferably
   applemint, finely chopped, plus
   several sprigs to garnish*

juice of ½ lemon

salt and ground black pepper

Place the figs in a pan with the wine and bring to a boil, then simmer very gently for about 1 hour. Leave to cool and refrigerate overnight.

Melt the butter in a pan and fry the turkey fillets until they are cooked through. Remove from the pan and keep warm. Drain any fat from the pan and pour in the juice from the figs. Bring to a boil and reduce until about ⅔ cup remains.

Add the marmalade, mint leaves, and lemon juice and simmer for a few minutes. Season to taste. When the sauce is thick and shiny, pour it over the meat and serve garnished with the figs and mint sprigs.

Desserts and Drinks

The digestive properties of mint make it ideal to round off a meal. Used sparingly, it can add an unexpected burst of flavor to fruit desserts and is excellent combined with chocolate and cream.

CHOCOLATE MINT TRUFFLE PACKETS

These exquisite little minted packets are utterly irresistible. There will be no leftovers.

Makes 18 packets

1 tbsp very finely chopped fresh mint

¾ cup ground almonds

2oz dark chocolate, grated

4oz crème fraîche or fromage frais

*2 dessert apples, peeled, cored
and grated*

9 large sheets filo pastry

⅓ cup butter, melted

*1 tbsp confectioner's sugar,
for dusting*

1 tbsp cocoa powder, for dusting

Preheat the oven to 375°F. Mix together the mint, almonds, chocolate, crème fraîche, and grated apples in a bowl. Cut the filo pastry sheets into 5in squares, and cover with a cloth to prevent them from drying out.

Brush a square of filo with melted butter, lay on a second sheet, brush again, and place a spoonful of filling in the middle of the top sheet. Bring in all four corners and twist to form a purse shape. Repeat to make 18 packets.

Place the filo packets on a cookie sheet well brushed with melted butter. Bake in the oven for approximately 10 minutes. Leave to cool and then dust with the confectioner's sugar, followed by the cocoa powder.

MINTED RASPBERRY BAVAROIS

A sophisticated dessert given extra elegance by the addition of fresh mint.

Serves 6

5½ cups fresh or frozen and thawed
    raspberries

2 tbsp confectioner's sugar

2 tbsp lemon juice

1 tbsp finely chopped fresh mint

2 sachets powdered gelatin

5 tbsp boiling water

1¼ cups custard

1 cup Greek-style yogurt

sprigs of fresh mint, to decorate

Reserve a few raspberries for decoration. Place the remaining raspberries, confectioner's sugar, and lemon juice in a food processor and process them until smooth. Press the purée through a strainer to remove the raspberry seeds. Add the mint. You should have about 2½ cups of purée.

Sprinkle 1 tsp of the gelatin over 2 tbsp of the boiling water and stir until the gelatin has dissolved. Stir into ⅔ cup of the fruit purée.

Pour this mixture into a 4-cup mold and leave the mold to chill in the refrigerator until the jelly is just on the point of setting. Tip the mold to swirl the setting jelly around the sides and then leave to chill until the jelly has set completely.

Stir the remaining fruit purée into the custard and yogurt. Dissolve the rest of the gelatin in the remaining water and stir it quickly into the custard mixture.

Pour the raspberry custard into the mold and leave it to chill until it has set completely. To serve, dip the base of the mold quickly into hot water and then turn it out, and decorate it with the reserved raspberries and the mint sprigs.

LEMON AND MINT CURD

Home-made lemon curd is infinitely tastier than the commercial variety. The addition of mint gives this version an interesting extra tang.

Makes about 3lb

6 fresh mint leaves

4 cups superfine sugar

1½ cups butter, cut into chunks

rind of 6 lemons, thinly pared, in large pieces, and their juice

8 eggs, beaten

COOK'S TIP

Try experimenting with different types of mint or substitute oranges for lemons. Lemon curd is best made using the freshest of ingredients, so buy new-laid eggs and try to find unwaxed lemons.

Place the mint leaves and sugar in a food processor and blend until the mint leaves are very finely chopped and combined with the sugar.

Put the mint sugar, butter, lemon rind, lemon juice, and eggs into a bowl and thoroughly mix together.

Set the bowl over a pan of simmering water. Make sure that it does not touch the surface of the water or the eggs will scramble. Cook, whisking gently, until all the butter has melted and the sugar has dissolved. Remove the lemon rind.

Continue to cook in this way, stirring frequently, for 35–40 minutes or until the mixture thickens. Pour into sterilized glass jars, filling them up to the rim. Seal with transparent covers or screw-top lids. Add a label and tie short lengths of string around the top of the jars to decorate. This lemon curd should be used within 3 months and once the jars have been opened, they should be stored in the refrigerator.

MINT JULEP

One of the oldest cocktails, this originated in the Southern States. Add fresh mint leaves according to taste. "Julep" is actually derived from an Arabic or Persian word, meaning rose water.

Serves 1

1 tbsp superfine sugar

8–10 fresh mint leaves

1 tbsp hot water

3 tbsp bourbon or whiskey

Place the sugar in a pestle and mortar, or in a bar glass with a muddler. Tear the mint leaves into small pieces and add to the sugar. Bruise the mint leaves to release their flavor and color. Add the hot water to the mint leaves and grind well together.

Spoon the mixture into a snifter glass or brandy balloon and half-fill with crushed ice. Add the bourbon or whiskey to the snifter glass. Stir until the outside of the glass has frosted. Allow to stand for a couple of minutes, to let the ice melt slightly and dilute the drink. Serve with straws, if liked.

Mint Julep is the most famous mint cocktail, but many others are also traditionally served with a mint sprig, especially those made with a base of crème de menthe. They include Green Devil (equal parts crème de menthe and vodka and the juice of ½ lime), Bloody Mary (vodka, tomato juice, Worcestershire sauce, lemon juice, cayenne pepper, and celery salt) and Czar's Delight (equal parts vodka and mint liqueur, light cream, and milk).

COOK'S TIP

Candied mint leaves (see page 11) make a pretty decoration for cocktail glasses, especially if you have frosted the rims with sugar first.

INDEX